# COLOUR IN ADVERTISING

# COLOUR
# IN ADVERTISING

## By Joseph Binder

LONDON: THE STUDIO LIMITED, 44 LEICESTER SQUARE, W.C.2

NEW YORK: THE STUDIO PUBLICATIONS INC., 381 FOURTH AVENUE

1 9 3 4

**STUDIO**

Reg. U.S. Pat. Off.

*Printed and Engraved in Great
Britain by Herbert Reiach, Ltd.,
43 Belvedere Road, London, S.E.1.*

# C O N T E N T S

# LIST OF PLATES

# LIST OF ILLUSTRATIONS IN TEXT

# ACKNOWLEDGMENTS

The Editors are indebted to the artists, advertisers and advertising agents from whose productions the colour plates in this book were made.

# FOREWORD

THE colour designs of "Arabia" coffee trade-mark, poster and package were specially executed by the author for this book, as also the arrangement of spectrum colours and the last of the set of four designs which demonstrate the use of black and red.

The others were originally selected for " Commercial Art and Industry " or for " Modern Publicity " because of some outstanding merit, and will already be known to subscribers to these publications. By re-issuing them in the present form several ends are served. It is possible to give a great profusion of colour illustrations, assembling together in compact form many of the best examples of contemporary colour advertising that have been produced, and to make their individual merits assist in a constructive explanation of the principles of colour.

# COLOUR IN ADVERTISING

# THE HARMONY OF CONTRASTS

## BY JOSEPH BINDER

### THE LAWS OF COLOUR

COLOUR is the poster-painter's chief means of creating effect. It is his vital factor, but for that very reason it is necessary in the first place to understand clearly what the laws of colour are. Nature has two forms of the visual, distinct from one another. The first is a row of non-coloured tones. This row begins with pure brilliant white and leads through countless inter-mediary stages—the various shades of grey — to the deepest black. We have spoken of a row, and there is good reason for this, for beyond the deepest black

11

and beyond the most brilliant white no further progress is possible. But in whatever ways these shades are mixed, colours can never be obtained from grey.

It is different with the coloured shades ; the real colours. If the single colours produced by the spectrum be placed side by side, then to be sure, a continuous row will also be formed, but this row has no end.

Yellow, if it is mixed with a little red, becomes orange, and if the yellow is gradually decreased, the orange becomes red. If blue is added to the yellow, it becomes green, and if the yellow is gradually removed from the green, it becomes blue. If a little red is added to the blue, then it becomes purple. If the blue is removed from the purple, it becomes red. That is to say, there is no limit to the row as is the case with the black-white scale ; it is a closed circle. In this colour-circle lies the secret of every colour-effect.

## COLOUR HARMONY AND THE POSTER

The poster-painter uses this effect as one of his strongest means of expression which helps him more than anything else to make the poster attractive. Therefore the colours which he uses for it must be harmonious. If they were not harmonious, people would be repulsed instead of attracted by the poster. But this harmony must not give a restful effect, for a rousing effect is the essence of a poster. It must challenge people to take an interest in something ; that is to say it must contain an inner tension which radiates out onto the contemplator.

And so we must specialise our demand for harmony in this way : it must be a harmony of contrasts, for only contrasts create tension, but the whole poster may be of one colour only, which may be a contrast to its surroundings.

The principle of colour-harmony is easy to grasp. Every artist and every business man can, with the help of the following lines, understand the laws of colour.

The well-known arrangement of colours according to the prism is not only physically correct, but it is also an arrangement which everyone feels to be

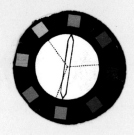

natural. If we place single colours as bits of paper in front of an unbiased person and ask him to arrange them, then he will always do so according to the prismatic colour-circle.

## PRISMATIC COLOUR

This prismatic colour-circle gives us the first explanation for the meaning of the harmony of contrasts, which we are striving to understand. If we imagine a straight line, movable like the hand of a clock, drawn through the centre of the circle, then the two ends of this straight line will always point to the contrasting or "complementary" colours, which together give a harmonious double accord, for instance, blue to yellow, red to green, orange to green-blue, yellow-green to violet. There are just as many intermediate shades between these main shades as there are points on the compass. If one wishes to obtain a harmony in three colours, then instead of a straight line through the centre of the circle three radii must be imagined, all inclined at the same angle of 12o deg. Every colour can be moderated from three points of view. The physicist Ostwald calls this the three-dimensionality of colour : The first dimension, as we have seen, is, that each colour is able to combine with another colour. For example : yellow and blue make green. The second dimension is that each colour can be mixed with white, the third, that each colour can be mixed with black. If complementary colours are mixed in the right proportions, then the result is grey. Here, the black-white row comes into

13

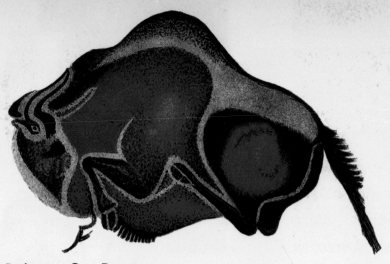

Prehistoric Cave Drawing

Greek Vase

contact with the colour-circle.  The mixing of the single colours with black or white determines their brightness or their darkness respectively.  The brightness or darkness of colours is the simplest means of representing space plastically.  For black and white correspond to the phenomena of light and shade, that is to say to modelling.  Impressionism for the first time consciously introduced these optical laws into art.  Manet, and even more his successor Monet, made use of the harmony of coloured contrasts, in order to give a direct impression of natural light (open air).  For that reason, impressionism renounces modelling in light and shade to a very large degree, and replaces it by a mosaic of complementary colours.  The co-operation of the contrasting colours stimulates the imagination of the contemplator to create for himself the illusion of space.

## STIMULATING THE EYE

We pause consciously at the word stimulation.  Because from here we have an easy and direct connection with the poster.  A poster must stimulate and it must occupy the eye ; consequently, it is an obvious idea to make use of the principle of impressionism for posters. The history of art shows that men have unconsciously gone in this direction.  The connections under con-

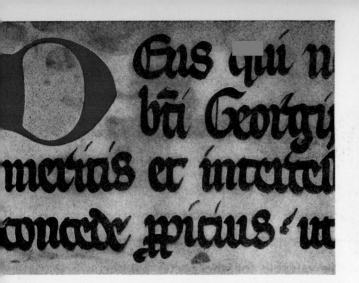

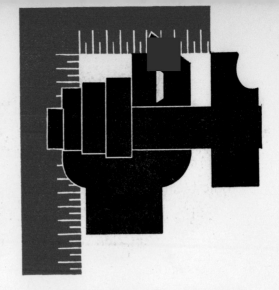

Manuscript                Advertising Design by Joseph Binder

sideration go beyond the mere achievements of art. For, simultaneously with the development of optics as a natural science, the development of modern life led to those forms of intercommunication in large towns which are well known to us all. Advertisement expanded suddenly, from modest beginnings. Posters were created, and that in the town where the modern life of a capital received its first universally valid stamp—in Paris. Here it was Jules Chéret, who developed the poster-style directly from impressionistic painting. He simplified the complicated system of small blobs and strokes of the brush—which in the paintings of impressionists were placed side by side like a mosaic—down to a clearly arranged ornament in the flat, comprehensible for every unprejudiced contemplator. A few systems of contrasting colours formed the basis of his composition. As a matter of fact, he did not go to the logical extreme, for, in the details, he kept to the drawings. It was his pupil and successor, Toulouse-Lautrec, who first found the courage to complete the conventionalisation of the surface consistently so as not to disturb the long-distance effect by petty details. Historically it was the discovery of Asiatic art which gave him the impetus for this. In the woodcuts of Hokusai he discovered the simple language of line and colour, which he then transferred to lithography. In England Nicholson and the Beggarstaff brothers almost reached the modern poster in their progress.

Up till now we have treated consciously only the optical side of the problem. The problem of the harmony of contrasts, however, has two other sides ; a physical and a psychological one. Though Newton explained the physical side of the matter, which we all learnt at school, the physiological and psychological representation is based on the much-rejected colour-doctrines of Goethe, which are nevertheless particularly valuable for the poster-painter. For the eye itself is not a physical apparatus. Whoever makes the simple experiment of painting a red spot on a piece of white paper and staring at it for a while and then spreading a piece of white paper over it will see a green spot in the place where the red one was. That is to say the eye itself is capable of producing colour. This experiment shows us that the laws of colour correspond to our innermost human disposition. We need green to free ourselves from the red. We need yellow to counterbalance blue. Now we also understand why the impressionists reckon with mere blobs of colour and from whence man takes the capacity to turn these blobs into a rhythmical colour scheme in his own imagination. Our eye is never idle, it co-operates ceaselessly to change the separate coloured details into an entity in our minds. The further we go in leaving out the connecting links between the colours, the bigger the part becomes, that falls to the eye of the contemplator, that is to say the interest of the contemplator is captured to the highest degree.

The recognition of this fact allows the poster-painter to obtain the most astonishing effects. These effects are also economical because they save a complicated process of work. Whoever really understand economy of colour can obtain the greatest effects with small means. Economy in poster-painting, as in everything else, is a sign of perfection.

# THE PSYCHOLOGICAL EFFECT OF COLOUR

The third form of colour-effect, which should not be underestimated by poster-painters, is the psychological effect. In the first place the law that is valid for the poster-painter is that he must characterise his subject by using normal colours in a pure and intensified manner. That is to say, for example, that he must paint a tree as powerfully and brilliantly green as possible. By means of this appealing to a general custom, he can obtain undreamt-of possibilities. These possibilities are particularly important for him, because he wishes to be forceful. He can paint an object in its contrasting instead of in its natural colours. Though, to be sure, he must be careful in doing this. If he were to paint bread blue, then it would be impossible to know what the painting was meant for. The change can only be carried through with such objects or creatures whose contours alone suffice to characterise them definitely for what they are. For example, a frog : no one seeing the silhouette of a frog will have any doubt as to what this outline is supposed to represent. A green frog in its natural colour will surprise no one. If, however, we paint the frog red then we intensify the effect of the picture. The eye, accustomed to fill in the silhouette of the frog with green, must make an effort to comprehend red here. So that if a person approaching a picture in the expectation of seeing a green frog is shown a red one, then he will be struck by the unnaturalness of the representation. From this we can see when the artist will be likely to employ such treatment, namely, whenever he wishes to obtain a surprising effect.

This means of creating effect in a poster was first tried in free art, namely in expressionistic painting. It happened about 20 years ago when the young generation sought a means of expression for their inmost feelings, which went further than mere naturalism. At that time it was discovered that an object could win an entirely new aspect by changing its colour. Franz Marc, a Munich painter, who was killed in the war, painted his famous picture " The Blue Horses," and the first expressionistic art society which he called to life in

17

Munich bore the programmatic name : the Blue Rider. The effect of this type of picture was pure amazement, even if it was amazement in a higher and, to a certain extent, in a metaphysical sense. One could feel something mysterious, without being able to solve the riddle. This incompletely developed experiment caused expressionism to come to an untimely end. For a picture must have a lasting and regular effect, as opposed to a poster, the sense of which is surprise and transitoriness. For that reason posters, which are merely enlarged pictures, are uneffective. Colour, however, apart from its primitive importance as local colour, has quite a different value. Everyone can experience for himself the various effects produced by different colours, quite apart from their importance for the subject of the picture. Yellow, which through its brightness is so akin to light, gives a warm and exciting effect. A room gains light if it is painted yellow, and the popularity of yellow curtains lies in the fact that even on dull days they give the illusion of sunshine. Therefore the poster-painter will employ yellow for certain definite psychological situations. But he must also bear in mind that yellow, as the colour of light, is most sensitive. Goethe, whom we follow in this, as in many other cases, knew that the addition of a little black sufficed to turn the optimistic character of yellow to pessimism.

In characterising further the main colours, we find that red strengthens yellow from the point of view of warmth. Not for nothing is it the colour of passion. It has an irritating effect on animals, and the use of red cloths for bull-fights in Spain is based on this fact.

Lastly, blue, the third basic colour, produces a feeling of peace and infinity. It seems to retreat from the eye, and to lead the spirit into never-ending distances. It is the colour of dreams and sleep. We can see this applied, as in a sleeping-car, where the night lighting is blue. The compound colour, green, which is composed of a mixture of blue and yellow, also holds the balance mentally between excitement and sleep. It is the most soothing colour ; most restful to the eye. That is the explanation for the psychologically soothing effect of a summer landscape which we have all experienced ourselves. Orange on the other hand, which is composed of optimistic yellow and

Designs by Joseph Binder for Trade-mark, Poster and Label for a grocer advertising coffee

passionate red, produces an expression of healthy activity. A mixture of peaceful blue and passionate red produces, on the contrary, an unbalanced effect. The disharmony and passivity of violet can also be interpreted as weakness. Every sort of goods has, as is the case in this example, its own colour determined either by tradition or by psychological effect. For example, bread—yellow corn-field ; laundry—blue, etc.

## THE SYMBOLISM OF COLOUR

Naturally, artists have always made the utmost use of these effects. In the fact that the madonnas of the old masters always wore blue coats lies a realization of the symbolism of colour, the attraction of which we can only feel indistinctly to-day. The poster-painter must revert to the symbolical meaning of colour ; for it leads to the deepest depths of the human soul. To be sure, it is left to his sense of tact to determine how much he shall exaggerate and change the natural colours, in order to bring the symbolism of his colour composition

19

to effect. If, for example, it is a case of making propaganda for a swimming pool, which should give a refreshing and at the same time a soothing effect, then the painter will be forced to work with the colour-circle from blue to green, whereby the objective idea of blue as the colour of water will assist him to complete the tension. He will also add a contrast which will appear in the colour-scale between yellow and red. The human body suggests itself naturally for this purpose, because the painter can intensify the colour of the skin to orange, which harmonises with the green and the blue, without distorting it unnaturally. We have grasped the fact that these psychological effects are also the most primitive for the fine arts. This assumption accords perfectly with the doctrine which the new science of excavation (the researches of pre-history) have revealed. The earliest colour that man used was black, obtained from coal dust, which is, as we have seen, a predecessor of true colour. It has no connection with the bright colours. The first bright colours to be used were the vegetable and mineral colours, which move between red and yellow. The paintings in the caves of the Ice Age, which we find in Spain, are attuned to the triple accord of red surface, black contour and white background, whereby modelling is effected by the grey-scale. This original and ever-effective colour accord reappears in the history of art in many distinctly important places. The most beautiful Greek vases are founded on the triple accord between the red colour of the pottery and the black and white of the painting.

When, in 1454, Gutenberg produced his first print, the famous bible of 42 lines, he printed the initials red. This colour harmony chosen by him has repeatedly proved itself to be the most effective in typography. What does this mean ? The very agreement between the three realms of art, so far apart as to time and material, which we have examined, can give us the explanation. It is in each case a question of decorative art in the flat. The first time it is a monumental style of art in the flat, the second time it is applied art in the flat, and the third time it is graphic art in the flat. The space-creating style of the illusionistic picture stands in opposition to this. Pictures would lose a lot were they to be reduced to such a simple colour harmony. During the period of the Secession such an attempt was made, but these pictures did not last long.

What is arbitrary in painting, however, is an inner necessity for decorative art. Here, simplicity is the chief means of creating effect. The modern poster can, to a certain extent, be regarded as the synthesis of all the styles we have mentioned. It is, like every frescoe, monumental as a result of its size. It is applied art, because it does not strive for illusionistic means, and it is typographical because it is printed, and because it seeks for the inner relationship to letters.

The triple accord black-white-red, that harmony of contrasts is, as it were, a guide through the labyrinth of modern poster-art.

It is the simplest contrast of harmonies, because it refers here not to the coloured-scale, but to the black-white scale, to the inner contrast of which, red gives a second contrast.

The master of poster-art will, of course, also make use of the more difficult contrast-harmony. But, however much he trusts to his imagination, he will never forget the everlasting laws which connect his work with productive nature.

## THE PRACTICAL APPLICATION

So much for the theoretical side. What does this process, the organisation of advertisement through colour, look like in practice ? Let us once again have recourse to a concrete example. A business man who wishes to start a wholesale grocery comes to the advertising-artist and asks for designs for his propaganda. The advertising-artist begins with the trade-mark, the first step in every such propaganda campaign. The latter must give a concentrated characterisation of the goods and protect them against imitation. We do not intend to go into detail as regards the drawing, but will only say this much : the composition of a trade-mark is similar to the historical development of writing. A pictorial conception is condensed to a formula. What interests us in this connection, the colouring of the trade-mark, is determined by the fact that the trade-mark must be effective in colour as well as in black and white, quite apart from the necessity of occasionally having to reduce it to a minimum in size. To return to the choice of colours for the trade-mark of the wholesale grocery we take a chief product, coffee, as our starting-point. For that reason we choose brown, because it is the local colour of roasted coffee, and to this green, the colour of the coffee-plant, is added as a decorative supplement. We use these two colours unbroken, so that their effect may be as strong as possible. And this leaves us in no doubt as to the execution of the technique. Only line-engraving comes into consideration, which either employs simple black or bright colours.

## CONSISTENCY IN THE COLOUR SCHEME

The second task for the artist to consider in his propaganda-campaign is a design for business-paper, that is to say for note-paper, bills, etc. In every case the trade-mark is the essence of the composition. But, next to the trade-mark, letters appear as a new element. We may regard as the first law for the treatment of colour in the letters the necessity of preserving in them the colour-accord which has already been used in the trade-mark.

The graphic-artist must design the names of the brands in characteristic letters, and this must be done in such a way as to allow these letters to be used as fixed formulae in every size and execution. The colour of the letters corresponds, as it does in the trade-mark, to the colour which has the strongest decorative effect, that is to say in our case, to green. The small letters which follow, consisting of the telephone-number, the telegraphic address, the banking-account, etc., must be kept small and can be written in typed letters. The colour of these small letters, is, logically, the second colour of the trade-mark, that is to say, brown. The technique for the paper is relief-printing for small editions. For large editions offset must be used.

## COLOUR AND THE PAMPHLET

The third task of the advertising artist is the arrangement of the prospectus. There are two possibilities here : The use of illustration and of letters ; it is, of course, taken for granted that the prospectus must contain pictures as well as text. The colouring of the prospectus must be consistent. Once more we use brown and green as the main colours. If other colours are used, then they must never play the most important part. The artist, if he draws the required pictures, should avoid delicate pen-strokes, and work with decorative surfaces. For only in this way is it possible to obtain the full effect of the colours. But the same law is also valid for photography. The photograph, a popular form of which is foto-montage, has a decorative value in relation to the page. It can be printed in, or in conjunction with colour and it must be printed like that if one does not wish to forego the propaganda-value of the colour-harmony once achieved. Green decorative surfaces will be added to foto-montage printed in brown which, in its turn, forms a rhythmical harmony with the brown lay-out of the letters. Within the text the name of the brand and the most important catch-lines are accentuated by green letters.

## COLOUR AND THE POSTER

Now, finally, we come to the most representative form of graphic propaganda, the poster. Nothing could be more mistaken, however, than to imagine that the poster is nothing but a prospectus enlarged to a monumental size. The means by which a poster achieves effect are fundamentally different. Here, it is long-distance-effect instead of near-effect. This means, as a matter of course, that the letters can only play a very secondary part. The poster is not read like a prospectus. The eye does not take in a series of communications one after the other, but it takes in the whole picture at a glance. The first necessity then for the coloured poster is simplicity. Simplicity, however, must not be commonplace. Each colour combination, even the simplest one, that the poster-painter arranges, must be original. It must be impressive, and must contain a maximum of expression. It would be wrong to imagine that the commercial graphic artist who has undertaken the propaganda for a wholesale grocery, must deviate from the brown-green harmony. On the contrary ; if he really wishes to impress the articles of his concern as unmistakably high-class goods on the public, then he must keep to it. Only he must not forget that every colour-effect is based on the proportion and composition of the coloured surfaces. The white of the paper which, from the point of view of printing technique, does not count as a colour, is, from an artistic point of view, a tremendously important means of increasing the colour-tension of the design. This means that a large number of bright colours does not necessarily increase the colour-effect. On the contrary, the effect as a whole can be flattened by it. Economy is the most important factor, here, as is always the case in modern poster art. For the contrasts between brown and green and green and white are stronger than if they were connected by intermediary shades. The half-shades, and this cannot be sufficiently stressed, are just as dangerous for the poster-painter as they are necessary for the painter of pictures.

So there must be no interchange of metiers. But the foremost law in advertisement is not only that one must keep to the colour-accord throughout, but also to the idea. From trade-mark to poster the fundamental idea must always remain the same. To be sure, it is just as wrong for a poster to be an enlarged trade-mark as it is for a trade-mark to be a miniature poster. The trade-mark is abstract—the poster concrete. The trade-mark is an idea which has been turned into a lifeless formula—a poster is an idea which has become a living reality. For example, the trade-mark of the wholesale grocery has been given a geometrically conventionalised figure, which to a certain extent gives the impression of hieroglyphs. The poster will retain as far as possible the fundamental scheme of this geometrical figure. But it will fill it with vitality. How does the artist achieve this ? His two chief means are individualising and modelling.

In the example shown the individualising will be as follows. The designer may turn the abstract figure into a plantation-worker carrying a bag of coffee

24

on his back.  Now, the difficulty in this process of individualisation lies in the fact that the primary geometrical form of the trade-mark figure must be preserved in the movements, without making the figure appear stiff.  The designer must therefore discover some form of movement which adapts itself to the geometrical style of the trade-mark design.

And now, as regards the modelling : In order to create an impression of reality, the artist must represent his figures plastically.  But he must never fall into the methods of the picture-painter and give the illusion of reality by filling the whole picture with a carefully worked-out colour- scheme.  Were he to do so, then he would ruin the proportion of the colour-elements, and above all, destroy the surface-effect of the poster.  There is, however, a simple means of overcoming this difficulty.  The poster-painter must, however much he owes to impressionism, renounce the impressionistic means of modelling. That is to say he must not dissolve his figure up in the various colours.  He must give up coloured reflections and shadows.  He will model his figures in the same way that, for example, the painters of the early renaissance (Boticelli) modelled theirs, namely with the help of the grey-scale.  First of all he must draw his figure in black and white, and then lay on the natural colour in transparent tones.  That is, so to speak, a school-example.  In our case, the poster-artist will start with the drawing in brown, on to which he will lay decorative green as a transparent layer.  In this way he achieves everything he wants ;  he has remained true to his brown-green harmony, and yet he has not destroyed the unity of the coloured surface-effect by impressionistic divisions, whilst at the same time he has obtained a plastic effect.  It is, however, most important that the plastic effect be confined to the figure, and not extended to the background.  If the background were treated plastically then the surface-effect of the poster-style would be destroyed. For small editions, lithography is used for reproducing posters, for large editions, offset.  The few words the poster contains should harmonise with the colour-effect of the poster.  The name and the trade-mark must also be repeated on the poster in the form and colour which have been chosen as permanent ; in this case it would be green.  The rest of the letters would be, logically, brown.  One can add as a general rule that the strongest effect with letters can be obtained by brilliant colour on a pale background.  If it is a question of very pale colours then the background must be given dark colour. Pale letters on a dark background have just as surprising an effect as the natural figures filled with unnatural colours which we have already mentioned. For the eye expects to see black, or at least dark, letters against the white of the paper.

## COLOUR AND THE PACKAGE

With the above-named, however, the task of a graphic artist in the service of advertisement is by no means exhausted.  All the goods of one and the same shop must have a uniform character in their equipment.  This does not mean by any chance that every single object must be packed in the same paper and boxes as every other one.  But there should and must be an artistic relationship between the various packings.  This relationship does not only consist of the obvious demand that each packing must bear the trade-mark, but, above all, that the same colour-harmony be used which was used for all the advertising devices of the firm.  One must not bring forward as an objection that our brown and green must necessarily lead to a dull and monotonous effect if is used for the various kinds of coffee-packings.  In this case the fertile imagination must produce attractive variations by continual new combination and distribution.  Coffee, when roasted, has a brown colour.  Were we to make the packing a bright brown as well, then the coffee would lose in conspicuousness and appear grey.  This consideration necessarily leads us to choose from the colours at our disposal, decorative green to contrast with brown for the principal colour of the packing.  By this means we obtain the contrasting harmony between the goods and the packing—the one enhances the effect of the other.  The proportion of the coloured surfaces belongs, as one of their most important factors, to the psychological laws of harmony.  This proportion

26

of colours consists of the coloured surfaces and the relative value of the shades of colours. Let us take the following practical example to illustrate the relative value of the shades of colours as proportion. If we take a black surface and a white surface and place an identical blue dot on each, then we see that on the white surface the blue dot has a dark effect whilst on the black surface it has a light effect. Besides this purely psychological result a second psychological result is also obtained, namely, the blue dot on the white gives a fresh bright impression whereas it has a sombre dynamic character on the black. This is, to be sure, only a very primitive example, but it shows that it is impossible to evolve any definite scheme for the use of colour, that is to say in the colour-composition. For all things connected with productive art can never be condensed to formulæ, as they would otherwise cease to be art and become science. The letters and the effect of the wrapper can be enhanced by various effects of material such as cellophane or metallic foil, without the necessity of making use of new and independent colours other than the brown and green harmony.

Up till now, for the sake of clarity in our description, we have kept strictly to our example, " coffee."

The grocer sells, apart from coffee, also cocoa, tea and other colonial productions. The goods are not only solid but also liquid. Countless variations result. A bottle which is filled with rum has a golden-brown effect. A comparatively expensive production has to be characterised on the label. We must therefore think out a new contrast ; the non-transparent object is opposed to the transparent one. Black has the most untransparent effect. To begin with, a black label will be conspicuous against the transparent contents of the bottle. But the costliness of the contents is still not expressed by this. We can best make it apparent by enlivening the black bottle with a rich ornament, which can, if desired, at the same time allude to the origin of the goods by all kinds of symbols. If we look out for a colour to be used for this ornament and stipulate that this colour must be striking and costly, then gold will suggest itself quite naturally. The text characterising the goods will be printed on a round coloured space. From old experience we choose red for the colour of this space, red with white letters. Here we make use of the time-old colour accord of black, white and red, already mentioned in our historical survey, which is still further enriched and enhanced by metallic gold, which is not a real colour. But there are also reasons for restraining the graphic artist from the free use of his imagination in designing wrappers. There are traditional reasons : Certain kinds of food, particularly those of overseas origin, have been brought to the market for hundreds of years in the original packing of the producer. For example, Chinese tea-caddies still impress the public. Such psychological effect must not be given up lightly, for that would be uneconomical. On the other hand, one must not insist on imitating, say, Japanese woodcuts. The modern graphic artist will only use the general colour impressions of the foreign original as the basis for his design to offset the technique in which his modern wrapper will be executed.

## THE NECESSITY OF STYLE

It must, however, always be borne in mind that an article determines the whole character of the shop. The artist who has been entrusted with the propaganda must be perfectly clear about this article. For his task is not really exhausted by the graphic creations which have occupied our attention up till now. To-day, business life knows no limit to advertisement. Everything must be saturated with the spirit of advertisement. For this reason the field of activity of the advertising artist is widened to that of a stage-manager. In the theatre the modern producer has to arrange everything, from the movements of the actors and the expression of their voices down to the lighting, the arrangement of the stage, the painting of the scenery and the background —in the same way that, say, a Max Reinhardt predetermines the whole style of the performance with the absolute power of a dictator, to use a decisive term. In this way also does the advertising artist determine the style of a business-concern.

The reader will ask : But has a business concern a style ? Is style not a form of art ? Most certainly every expression of life has its own style and so also does that highest and most intense expression of life represented by modern business-life. There is a Henry Ford style just the same as a Louis XIV style. There is a style for grocery. And there is not only a style for grocery in general, but every really smart and successful grocer has his own personal and unmistakable style which he presents to the public.

Much is necessary for that ; wrappers and headings, yes, and even posters are mere details when viewed from such an angle. It is necessary to communicate the impetus of business life to the outer world. But, to return to our school example, this impetus lies in the tension between the two colours, green and brown. And so everything concerning this business will be green and brown. The green and brown of the wrappers will determine the interior of the shop ; externally decorative green will be used as tiles in the porch. The liveries of the salesmen and errand-boys will be brown and green. The vans for delivering the goods will also be brown and green. And so the colour of the coat of arms of the modern merchant will become part of the whole aspect of a town, and by trading his goods his business style will even be carried out into the world. Branches in foreign towns will bring the style of the head-firm before the eyes of the population, and to the furthest corners of the earth the sound of the trade-mark will evoke a certain definite colour-association which has, at the same time, the psychological effect of attesting to the quality. Just as Ariadne's thread led Theseus through the labyrinth, so will the colour of the modern merchant's coat of arms lead the consumer to his shop.

JOSEPH BINDER

# PLATES

# PLATE I

## ELMER O. TETZLAFF

Cover of a folder in colours for
the Meyer-Rotier-Tate Co.


# PLATE I A

## EDOUARD BENITO

Cover of a folder in colours for
Stehli Silks

## EFFECTS GAINED BY BROAD SURFACES AND BY COLOUR PATTERN

The original folders are examples of water-colour printing in flat tones—a method which can be employed in letterpress printing with brilliant results.

These two plates effectively demonstrate two different uses of colour. At the top broad surfaces and in the lower colour pattern. Here they are reproduced by the half-tone colour process. The top illustration could be equally well reproduced in colour-line in four printings, which would reduce the cost of cuts or blocks. Both could be reproduced by lithography.

1.—" Head of an Indian." At the first glance the effect is striking. The reason is, that the artist has used a contrast between two complementary colours : red and green, and has set off these complementary colours against one another in clear simple surfaces. The head of the Indian is a black silhouette in front of the white background, and by means of this an effective contrast is again obtained. Further the eye is particularly drawn to the contrasts by a skilful drawing of the lines. (Bow and arrow.)

1a.—In this case the task is slightly different than for a poster. It does not depend so much on long-distance effect as on an attractive filling of the surface. For that reason the composition can and must be more complicated than it is in a poster. Therefore the artist has made the dress of the figure out of tiny surfaces pieced together like a mosaic. That would only be a drawback for long-distance effect, but for a small design this complexity is an enrichment. The danger of restlessness is cleverly avoided. The artist is fully conscious of the importance of the proportions of the coloured surfaces for his artistic ends.

# PLATE 2

**GEORGES HORDYNSKY**

Decorative Illustration

## GEOMETRICAL TREATMENT OF A DESIGN IN TWO COLOURS

A strictly geometrically conventionalised figural composition which clearly shows cubistic influences. The artist confines himself to one colour : Yellow. He places this colour in clear simple surfaces on a white background and adds black rhythmical surfaces and lines to it. The advantage of this simplicity is obvious. Nowhere does the surface of the drawing appear indefinite. Everything can be clearly perceived at the first glance. The contrasts imprint themselves on the mind.

This is one of the simplest forms of the use of colour, and one of the least expensive to reproduce. For a small-sized plate it could be reproduced either by lithography or in line, the cheaper form of process reproduction. In either case only two printings are required. The paper stock used need not be expensive and a wide selection is possible. It would have been possible, had it been so desired, to use a coloured-paper stock, but in that case care would have been necessary in the choice of the colour, as the yellow printing would be affected by the colour of the paper.

# PLATE 3

**TOM PURVIS**

Poster for Austin Reed Ltd.

## THE PLAYFUL USE OF COLOUR

What is at first sight an ornamental riband of red turns out on inspection to be a worm—which the early bird catches. The colour is a gay and, in this sense, " playful " adjunct to the bold lettering.

It is almost possible to say that the idea, which was one of the most successful of its kind, could not have been put over without the colour. In black and white, the advent of spring with its brighter days would have been much more difficult to put over, and without that the sales appeal would have been reduced enormously.

The effect depends on two kinds of contrast. First of all on the complementary pair of colours green and red, and secondly on the composition in diagonals. The bird with its tail and its beak forms a diagonal line from the top left-hand side down to the bottom right-hand side. This line meets the letters at right-angles and they form another diagonal. The beak, which is accentuated by its red colour, has a second function as well : it draws attention to the most important row of letters and is supported in this by the expression in the eye.

# PLATE 4

## HANNS WAGULA

Poster for the Adriatic Town
of Dubrovnik

## COLOUR EXPRESSIVE OF WARMTH AND DISTANCE

Atmosphere is the essential thing to be conveyed here. Here are warmth, sunlight, an atmosphere of health and pleasure, a comforting place to rest in, all conveyed to the mind by colour.

The artist's task was to make a poster for a town on the Adriatic. The main colour, the blue of the sea, was already determined by that. The artist, who has a fine feeling for colour, has as a result used the complementary colour yellow, in the landscape. He uses the red roofs to accentuate the composition and opposes them with a neutral grey-brown in the foreground. This composition would have no long-distance effect if the artist had not indicated the vegetation by black silhouettes. By this means the picture obtains depth as well as an ornamental division.

# PLATE 5

## HERMANN KOSEL

Poster for Artists' Colourmen
Kaspar & Co.

## THE SHOCK POSTER

A typical example of startling effect. A red mannikin which symbolises the colour. As a contrast to the unnatural colour of this human figure, the bottle drawn in indian ink is kept deep black. By this means the character of the goods, for which propaganda is being made here, is particularly clearly characterised. Here as well the harmony of contrasts is used throughout.

To the red of the mannikin in oil-colour is opposed green. The black of the bottle stands out against the white of the background. The yellow of the stopper of the bottle and of the label are complementary to the blue of the cap and of the globe. Various browns in the letters and in the tube act as intermediaries.

# PLATE 6

## FUNK

Swiss Resort Poster

## COLOUR USED FOR EMPHASIS IN A GEOMETRICAL DESIGN

Colour produced the effect. Convert it into black and white and the atmosphere conveyed would of necessity be very different and much less effective. The contrasts and bold flat colours ensure interest from a considerable distance.

The picturesqueness of an old town in Switzerland is conveyed by using colour in quaint geometrical patterns. The artist uses a conventionalisation for this which has its origin in children's toys. By this means he obtains striking simplicity. To make these simple forms effective for a poster, he attunes them to the fundamental accord black and white. But seeing that this harmony of non-coloured tones would have a dead effect in such a simplified drawing, he brings life into the whole by adding red and other bright-coloured surfaces which form geometrical figures and stand in rhythmical connection to one another.

# PLATE 7

**HERALD REPRODUCTION CO.**

Showcard for Abraham and
Straus, N.Y.

## CREATING ATMOSPHERE

It is very hot, but here is comfort and cool shade. These are people who take a pride in themselves and their home and have a social status and a standard of taste. All of this is said by colour : the predominance of red also calls attention to the important part which " Summer Home Furnishings " play in the scheme of things.

The sunny effect of this design is obtained by the yellow, the colour of the sun. A very light green is used as a complementary colour to this very light yellow, which enhances the friendly character of the whole " atmosphere." The shadows are also light and the red, which strikes one most, has its brilliance increased by yellow. The plastic effect which is endangered by the lack of dark tones for the shadows, is achieved by a very skilful diagonal composition with interlacing of these single elements of the picture.

SUMMER HOME

FURNISHINGS

# PLATE 8

## M. E. ANGERER

Poster for the British
Railways

## EFFECT GAINED BY THE RHYTHMICAL REPETITION OF COLOUR

The artist's problem was to present in one poster the idea of many different countries. This he has done by using small figures in which colour indicates local costume.

If small reproductions on short runs were required the silk-screen process would be useful.

The composition is arranged according to typographical principles in this railway-poster. The figures are standing on stripes which in their turn are spaces for the letters. The artist deviates from the use of complementary colours, but the contrast between blue and red, which he uses chiefly, is yet strong enough to divide up the surface. The most important feature in the poster is the rhythm of the figures throughout, which is accentuated by skilful division of coloured and white surfaces.

# THE CONTINENT

## BY

## 14 ROUTES

DOVER - CALAIS
DOVER - OSTEND
FOLKESTONE - BOULOGNE
FOLKESTONE - DUNKERQUE
NEWHAVEN - DIEPPE
SOUTHAMPTON - HAVRE
SOUTHAMPTON - ST. MALO

HARWICH - HOOK
HARWICH - FLUSHING
HARWICH - ANTWERP
HARWICH - ZEEBRUGGE
HARWICH - ESBJERG
HULL - ZEEBRUGGE
GRAVESEND - ROTTERDAM

For all information apply Continental Departments LIVERPOOL STREET STATION, E.C.2 (for Harwich Routes),
or VICTORIA STATION, S.W.I (for Southern Routes), or any Station, Office or Agency of the

# GWR · LNER · LMS · SR

# PLATE 9

## E. McKNIGHT KAUFFER

Poster for Shell-Mex Ltd.


# PLATE 9 A

## ERIC FRASER

Booklet cover produced
by the Central Advertising
Service Ltd. for Gordon Hotels Ltd,

## THE COUNTERCHANGE OF COLOURS
## IN POSTER LETTERING

Poster for Shell in conjunction with an aeroplane exhibition. The fuel itself is made known by the internationally famous name. For this reason the letters play the most important part in the composition. The letters are treated in colour in a very skilful way, namely, by making use of the strongest contrasting effects. It must be noted : the letters are partly white on a coloured background and partly coloured on a white background. An aeroplane simplified almost to a trade mark, draws attention to the character of the exhibition.

" Shell," the name of the product, in solid black on a yellow ground, dominates the design without definitely indicating one national flag ; the rectangles of colour suggest the flags of several nations. The lighter blue streaking behind the aeroplane suggests speed.

A poster of this kind uses much less ink than one where the colours spread over the whole area.

## HISTORICAL ATMOSPHERE

Nothing blatant could be associated with " Mayfair," which prides itself on correctness and tradition. The designer has made full use of these two qualities by the quiet dignity and old-world charm of his colouring of figures and background.

INTERNATIONAL

SHELL

VISIT STAND NO 10
SECTION 6

AERO EXHIBITION 1909

"MAY FAIR"

LONDON MCMXXX

# PLATE 10

## MICHEL BOUCHAUD

Poster Advertising Monte Carlo

## SUNSHINE SUGGESTED BY LIGHT TONES OF COLOUR

Compare this poster with plate four, where the problem is much the same but stronger colours have been used. Here, the figures in the foreground play an important part by their suggestion of a fashionable exclusive resort, and the fame of " Monte Carlo " has not been overlooked in arranging the lettering at the base.

The sunniness of the landscape is obtained by keeping all the colours in the most delicate shades. The human figures are emphasised by allowing them to cut vertically into the landscape composition.

# PLATE II

**JOSEPH  BINDER**

"Give Books" Poster

## EFFECT GAINED BY DECORATIVE LETTERING
## ON BANDS OF COLOUR

Three-colour poster with white letters on coloured and black surfaces. The arrangement is strictly linear. A maximum of coloured effect is obtained by variations between black and white. All representation is left out. The whole attention is drawn to the conception of the book. Only a laurel leaf appears as a symbol of literature.

An economical but effective result can be obtained by the use of lettering only, as is shown in this three-colour poster.

WÜNSCHT EUCH

BÜCHER

DER TAG DES

BUCHES

22. MAERZ 1929

SCHENKT EUCH

BÜCHER

# PLATE 12

## KATO LUKATS

Showcard for Cosmetics

## EMPHASIS ON COLOUR THAT SYMBOLISES THE PRODUCT

Colour is used simply to give the effect of charm and freshness proper to the cosmetics advertised. With only two colours a very complete and yet economical effect is obtained.

The line work is graceful, and an economic use of black gives an ornamental support to the otherwise all-too-delicate harmony. White suggests powdered face and hair.

This is another subject in which water-colour inks could be used.

# PLATE 13

**HALLMAN**

Poster for a Swedish Cinema

## VIVACITY PRODUCED BY BROKEN PATCHES
## OF COLOUR ON WHITE GROUND

In this Swedish cinema poster the aim has been to symbolise the film, thus giving attention in a way that a still photograph could not hope to do.

The white paper is made to do a great deal by the judicious placing of the colour, with consequent saving of ink, an important matter in posters of large size.

Contrary to the usual type of photographic drawing, the artist does not even try to compete with cinematography. He gives up the illusionism of photography, but he consciously makes use of that form of expression, which is unobtainable for cinematography, namely colour.

The effect of the poster lies in the first place in the harmony of the contrasting colours yellow and blue, which we already know from so many examples, as well as the non-coloured shades black and white. To this double contrast red appears again to accentuate the composition and brown is used as an intermediary shade. The drawing makes use of subtle means. The single colour-surfaces form complicated groups which are subordinate to a diagonal main direction. But the proportions of these colour surfaces are so skilfully calculated as to give a strong long-distance effect to the whole.

# PLATE 14

**MICHEL BOUCHAUD**

Menu cover for Les Grands
Magasins du Bon Marche

## MELLOW COLOURING USED TO GIVE
## OLD-WORLD EFFECT

A menu-card is a special problem in which the artist may be inspired by something appropriate to the particular occasion or by something purely fanciful.

Here the design illustrates a refrain, the music and words of which are printed on the first inside pages of the menu, the mellow colours suggesting a romantic and old-world feeling.

The " pochoir " processes could be used for a design of this kind.

BON VOYAGE CHER DUMOLLET

# PLATE 15
## JEAN DUPAS
Fashion Drawing

## STYLE ACHIEVED BY LIMITATION OF COLOUR

This is a two-colour half-tone reproduction made for " Commercial Art and Industry " from an original drawing. Nothing is wasted. Although there are only two printings, many tones and shades have been obtained at an economical cost.

The artist's aim is the utmost elegance of effect. For this reason he leaves out all colour contrast and attunes his picture entirely to brown. He uses a naturalistic drawing only slightly conventionalised. He accentuates the exotic character of the woman he represents by indicating a fantastic landscape with palms.

# PLATE 16

## ALEXEIEFF

Poster for the London and
North Eastern Railway

## DREAM-LIKE EFFECT OF MERGING AND SUBDUED COLOURS

The idea of a night-express takes a fairy-like form in the imagination of the artist. He allows the engine to float like some vision between mountains, water, moon and stars. The colours merge into one another so that all the contrasts are as far as possible, softened. In spite of this, however, the contrasts are there, as can be seen by the presence of pink in the sky and green in the foreground. But these contrasts are to a certain extent hidden, which gives a strange atmosphere to the whole.

The suggestion of floating effortlessly along is cleverly conveyed.

" Travel while you sleep " certainly comes through. There is nothing in it to suggest that your dreams will be either unpleasant or disturbed.

# PLATE 17

## H. S. WILLIAMSON

Poster for London's Underground

## THEATRICAL COLOUR

To suggest the excitement and merriment of a theatrical performance the artist has used the methods of a " straight " oil painting in which decorative effect is retained by the dominance of red and white. He has succeeded, with the aid of colour and his placing of the lettering, in linking the rhythm and colour of the theatre with the idea of using the Underground to get to and from the show, which was not an easy proposition.   The lure of the theatre itself has been used to sell railway tickets.

## FORM INDICATED BY COLOUR

The roundness and solidity of the tree trunks, the mass of the foliage so refreshing to the eye of the town-dweller, is given by the colour itself in the manner of the modern picture painters of the post-impressionist school.

Again the essential thing conveyed by the colour is atmosphere. However clever the artist might be it would be impossible to produce equally compelling suggestions of the freshness and beauty of the countryside had colour been omitted.

This is Ashtead Woods, served by Route 65 from Ealing Broadway Station.

# Route 144ᴮ Caterham Valley

# From Elephant & Castle Stn. (Sundays only)

Another **GENERAL** Busway

## COLOUR PHOTOGRAPHY USED TO CREATE
## THE ILLUSION OF REALITY

From the advertiser's point of view the photograph is unequalled as a convincing illustration of his product, and colour greatly enhances the selling value. A colour photograph can be used to bring about a maximum of illusion-istic effect. It will be used particularly in cases where manifold coloured objects have to be represented in detail. In our case the gaily coloured heads of the matches are taken as the principal motive for the representation. A suitable drawing of the lines draws the attention to the coloured shimmer of the heads of the matches. A non-coloured background would still further increase the coloured effect of the principal motive.

This illustration was reproduced by colour half-tone. It could also be done in colour-gravure, and for short runs where quality was more important than cost colour-collotype would have also been possible.

## DETAILS UNITED BY COLOUR

This is an example of the use of two broad surfaces of contrasting colour, with the addition of very slight touches of an additional colour at top and base, the lighter colour being broken up by the pattern obtained by the serial plan. It will be noticed that all the detail is confined to the yellow area, in the shape of the historical coat of arms of the city of Munich, so that the black stone would be very easy to prepare for lithographic reproduction.

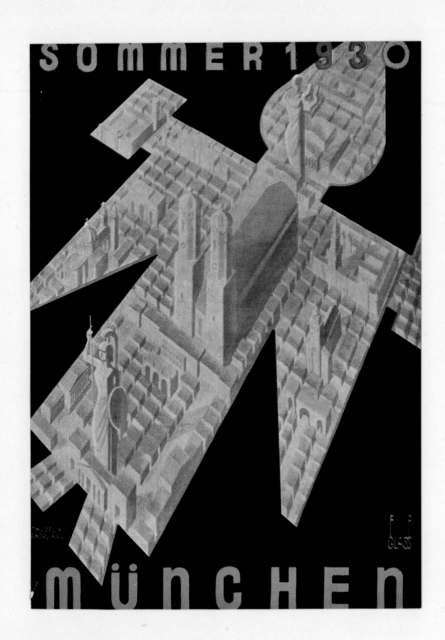

# PLATE 21

**ROBERT BERENY**

Poster for Modiano Cigarettes

## BALANCE OF COLOUR

In this poster, colour is used for surface value only and a careful counter-poising of values can be noticed. The striking red of the hand has, without doubt, the strongest effect in the drawing and shows up the object advertised in white. Blue serves to balance the black, and the figure is treated in such an abstract manner that it only appears as a silhouette.

# PLATE 22
## AUBREY HAMMOND
Posters for "232" Grey Flannels

## COLOUR SYMBOLISM

A comparison of these two showcards for flannel demonstrates very clearly the advantages of colour. In both cases the main lines of the design are similar, yet by the use of colour totally opposite effects have been obtained. In the one, a rhythmical treatment of the lines and the avoiding of colour contrasts gives the monotonous impression of rain, while yellow and red, the colours for light and warmth, have been used in a conventionalised manner in the other example.

In both cases only three printings have been used.

# PLATE 23

## "CUB" OF GREENLYS LTD.

Trade Sign for Don Ltd.

## COLOUR IN THE SHOP SIGN

Again, the much-used principle of placing bright colours on a black surface has been employed and its value here, as a background for colour, is obvious, as is also the difference between the advancing warm colours and the receding cold. Proportionately to area, comparatively little of any colour except black is required.

# PLATE 24

## LOUPOT

Poster for Valentine Paints

## BROKEN COLOUR AS A BACKGROUND

This poster for colours themselves makes use of a background of natural brush marks. By means of a good proportional division the shades green, blue and red have an exceptionally lively effect and are joined to form a closed surface by the intermediary black in the centre. Although the colours are on a white ground, the artist has obtained an increased effect of white in the figure which is drawn in white lines. From this example we see once more the advantage of plenty of white space.

# Where men count the most

In the process-engraving house, efficient, up-to-the-minute plant is naturally an asset to the execution of good work. But men count the most. ¶ The making of a process plate requires a long series of steps, each necessitating the work of the highest type of skilled craftsmen. Every job is a different job. No two are exactly alike in any particular. Infinite experience and unerring discretion are vital. ¶ Buy your process-engravings from Nickeloid; where the combination of carefully picked men and machinery works, under skilled direction, to produce engravings as near perfection as it is humanly possible to accomplish.

Send for details of Nickeloid service and specimens of everyday work. The Nickeloid Electrotype Co. Ltd., Printer St. London, E.C.4

# NICKELOID

## THE HOME OF CRAFTSMEN

| Date Due | | | |
|---|---|---|---|
| Loan | | | |
| DEC 6 '48 | | | |
| Loan | | | |
| MAR 20 '61 | | | |
| MAY 1 0 1960 | | | |
| FEB 1 1 1962 | | | |
| JA 5 '64 | | | |
| '8 | | | |
| JA 26 '65 | | | |
| FEB 1 1 1969 | | | |
| | | | |
| MAY 2 1 1969 | | | |
| MAY 2 1 1969 | | | |
| | | | |
| | | | |
| | | | |
| | | | |
| | | | |